MAKE YOUR OWN BREAK: HOW TO MASTER YOUR VIRTUAL MEETING IN SEVEN SIMPLE STEPS

Jennifer Lieberman

Maple Mermaid Publishing Corporation

HOW TO MASTER YOUR VIRTUAL MEETING IN SEVEN SIMPLE STEPS

STEP #1   MAGIC IN THE LIVING ROOM

STEP #2   SET UP (TO WIN) i - LOCATION

STEP #3   SET UP (TO WIN) ii - LIGHTING

STEP #4   SET UP (TO WIN) iii - FRAME

STEP #5   APPEARANCE

STEP #6   MENTAL PREP

STEP #7   PRESENTATION

STEP # 1

MAGIC IN THE LIVING ROOM

Our world has evolved into this incredible global community. Thanks to the technological advances of our time we can travel the world and have face-to-face conversations with family, friends and colleagues thousands of miles away without ever leaving our living room. The evolution of technology has afforded us experiences that were never possible one or even two decades ago. We are able to communicate in real time with anyone, anywhere in the world, at any time of day. How cool is that?

The benefits of these capabilities are countless and as we become more adept with this type of communication, the more we have become reliant on it for our businesses and work efficiency. Like everything, along with the positives there are a few less positive aspects of the business world going virtual; some of us feel a little lost. It's okay, you're not alone.

Many of us feel more self-conscious on camera than when we are physically in front of the people we are meeting with for a pitch, presentation, board meeting, brainstorming session or even a simple work check in. Many of us feel that our office environment fuels us towards success and are unsure of how to connect powerfully and leave an impact during a virtual meeting. That's why I wrote this book; using my expertise as a professional actor, producer and director I have many on-camera tips and tricks to share to help you *master your virtual meetings*.

Over the past five years I've heard many professional actors lament that the majority of their auditions are now "self-tapes", where the actor must record the audition on their own, losing out on meeting the casting directors, directors or producers in person. It can feel like a missed opportunity. Also, the onus is now on the actor to have a suitable **shooting setup** and another actor to read the lines opposite them; in the past these things were provided at the audition at the expense of the people doing the hiring.

As much as there is a benefit to an in person meeting/audition, there are also countless benefits to a "self-tape" or **virtual meeting** because the individual has much more control over their environment. As actors have learned to 'lean in' to the new world of auditions, so will business professionals with virtual meetings.

The most important aspect of success is *feeling* successful, in this book I'll help you set yourself up both physically and mentally to succeed in your virtual meetings with seven simple steps.

The difference between a live in-person meeting and a virtual one is that for the virtual meeting we are in a perpetual "close up" shot, in contrast to a fuller environment with more visual diversions. I like to compare this to the difference between a stage performance and on-camera acting. Although the basic principles of performing are the same across both mediums, film acting requires a few different techniques and a completely different set-up for it to be effective. I've been working in both film and theatre for almost two decades and understand the distinct differences between the two mediums.

As the business world has become more reliant on virtual interactions I've been approached by professionals and executives to specifically help make their *virtual presence* more effective by transferring principles from the film acting and directing world. In the process of coaching these individuals I came up with a simple seven-step approach and was encouraged to write this book to help others by making the steps easily accessible .

Before any script hits a stage (or sound stage) there are many steps to get there, but they all start off with the same thing, I like to call it *magic in the living room*. Whether you're a writer creating a story, a director bringing a world to life or an actor breathing air into a character, all the work starts in your own living room...and if you can't "bring it" there, you'll never get a chance to "bring it" anywhere else. For most creatives this is a given because we don't normally have a consistent office, studio or theatre to go to; we will be in one place for the extent of the gig and then move on to the next location. The only consistency we have with our work is in our living room.

As more business professionals are working from home, the *magic in the living room* becomes an important concept to embrace. I use the word *living room* loosely, you may have a home office, or like working on your bed, or at the kitchen table, the specifics aren't important, but the concept is the same. Making the *magic* at home is key...creating an environment conducive to success wherever you happen to be is the real talent. And since the *magic* is in you, you can make it happen anywhere!

STEP #2

SETUP - LOCATION

Now that you are aware of the task; *to make magic in your living room* (home office, kitchen, or whatever room best suits your needs) let's address some of the visual aspects of setting yourself up for success:

The goal for your setup is to look *polished and professional* with minimal visual distractions so your colleagues and clients can stay focused on you and what you are saying. I know this isn't what you signed up for, you probably didn't pursue a career in broadcast, but resisting where the future is going will only leave you behind. I'm gonna keep it pretty simple, I promise. And in the long run, if you follow these steps, you'll be so ahead of the game, I bet some unexpected opportunities might even come your way.

There are three major aspects of your setup: **location**, **lighting** and **frame**. In this chapter we will discuss **location**. Choosing a **location** with a suitable **background** isn't as simple as you may think. There are a few things you need to take into consideration.

First, you want to choose a space with good **natural light**. We will get into the specifics of the lighting setup in step #3, but having a space with good natural light will help with lighting in general.

Second, you want to be sitting on a proper **hardback chair**, a sofa or soft chair is out of the question. You will need a proper chair where you can sit upright on your sits-bones with your feet planted on the ground; this active position is also an activating position. You will want to be angled forward in the chair ready for action, not leaning back, lounging in a passive position. There is a huge energetic difference connected to your posture (thanks mom) and believe me, it comes through on the camera.

Standing is also an option if you have a standing desk and if you feel more energetic on your feet. However, if you do decide to stand watch out for getting fidgety, leaning on the desk, shifting your weight from side to side, rocking back and forth - all these movements can come across negatively on camera as tired, bored or disinterested and the movements can be very distracting. We all have physical habits we are unaware of that can be magnified when on camera, so now is a good time to become super aware of your physicality.

Third is the actual **location** that will be behind you and visible to the camera. You will want to have a clean and straight-forward **background**. It is best to avoid mess, clutter, busy and distracting patterns. A plain color wall can work well. Bookshelves seem to be quite popular and send a professional message. Sitting in front of a window is not a good option, the light coming in from the window will be behind you and make your face appear too dark.

What mood are you trying to evoke? Think of a few words of how you would like to be perceived in your meeting, write them down and use them as a reference to how you set up your space. Authoritative? Insightful? Inspiring? Empowering? Caring? Powerful? Trustworthy? Compassionate? Get specific!

I believe the **background** to be a fantastic opportunity to tell a story about yourself visually and set a specific tone, like a director does on camera. In the film world everything on set is specifically curated to help tell the story: the colors of the walls, the styles of artwork and types of furniture used. All these elements work together with lighting to create a mood and reveal details about the characters and places we are seeing.

What story would you like to tell about yourself and your business?

Don't get ahead of me. I'm not saying you need to buy new furniture, paint or redecorate your space, but there are some subtle changes you can make that can speak volumes.

The type of background that will be effective for you depends on the type of meeting you will be having. If you will be meeting with colleagues your goals will be different than if you will be meeting with clients. The information you share visually will be more relevant to someone you are meeting with the first time or second time, than if you are engaging with someone you have a long history with compared to someone you meet with daily or weekly.

We all take visual cues from our environment that help us connect in a meeting. Having some personal photos of family, a pet, or an activity you frequent offers opportunities to engage on a personal level. A souvenir of a place you traveled to, an achievement outside of your work, a painting you like, an inspiring quote or a stack of your favorite books in the background can reveal some information about you and opens the door to a more personal connection. We all prefer to do business with people we can relate to on a human level and even have some things in common with. You may also want to have a company logo or slogan somewhere visible.

Don't stress if you don't have the space to curate your background, it's not imperative. A plain wall will do just fine. If need be you can even use a solid colored sheet preferably blue or gray (with no wrinkles) and tack it up behind you using push pins to give you a clean background. Place a small end table in front of the sheet either to the left or right of your chair, place a photo and a stack of books and presto, fabulous curated background. That's even simple enough to pull together 30 minutes before your meeting. The most important thing is that the location looks neat and professional.

Please, please, please **do not** use a virtual background unless you have a proper *green screen* (literally a green screen or sheet hanging behind you, these were invented specifically for CGI, computer generated imaging, so you can drop in whatever background you wish making it appear in a realistic manner). I've had clients insist they could skip this step because they had a virtual background and this was always a disaster. First, a virtual background only works if you have a proper *green screen*. Otherwise parts of your face, ears, hair, hands and other body parts are constantly disappearing and this is distracting, not to mention comes across as unprofessional. Second, a virtual background comes across as insincere, which can work against you in a virtual meeting where you want to be perceived as authentic. You are already missing out on a *real* connection, so authenticity is key in your virtual meetings. Third, many times your colleagues and clients become sidetracked wondering where you actually are and what your true setting looks like.

The story you want to tell may change depending on the meeting, if this is the case, it's a good idea to have a few different accent pieces (photos, souvenirs, artwork) handy that you can swap out in order to be specific to who you're meeting with.

See, that wasn't too bad, right? And now that you have some specific guidance I'm sure you're gonna come up with something awesome!

Questions to consider:

What story are you telling about yourself?

What story are you telling about your business?

Who are you meeting with?

What is the tone of this meeting?

How would you like to be perceived?

Does your background enhance, detract or distract from it?

STEP #3

SETUP - LIGHTING

Why is **lighting** even important? Although no one expects you to go out and invest in a professional lighting setup, lighting does set a specific tone and mood. Don't let bad lighting cast a shadow over your presentation. Very quickly the virtual meeting has moved from the exception to the norm in daily business life. That is why it's important to learn to work with what you have...or invest in some basic equipment to make your life easier in the long run.

I know the idea of a **lighting setup** can be daunting and that lighting probably isn't even something you've thought of before beyond the on and off switch (unless setting the mood for a romantic encounter). I get it, and it's really not that hard to grasp once you put a little bit of effort into it.

It's important to be well lit during your virtual meeting because your colleagues and clients need to see you clearly, especially your eyes. Clear eye contact is key to clear communication and a successful meeting. Ultimately doing this correctly will only take a few minutes of your time in order to achieve the huge benefits of looking wonderfully professional.

What seems like enough light in life isn't always enough for the camera because of where the light is coming from or the angle it hits you. Insufficient or improper lighting can come across as moody and low energy, you definitely don't want that. It is also harder to see your eyes clearly when you're not lit well and

This is a great time to refer back to the words you wrote down in the last chapter about how you want to be perceived. I'm almost positive that bright, clear lighting will compliment what you are going for.

Relying on natural light from the window or whatever overhead and lamp lighting are already in your chosen location are not always the most effective choices. Unless you're a professional actor, YouTuber or Instagram model, chances are when you set up your living space you most likely didn't have on-camera lighting (for business meetings) on your mind. Don't sweat it, in this step we will go over some useful tips to make sure you are well lit for your meeting.

If you have a nice window that gets a lot of natural light try and set up your **location** facing that window. If facing the window head on is not an option, try to angle yourself as close to the window as you can. Of course the amount of light coming in will depend on the weather and time of day, that's why you will not rely solely on this light source.

I suggest investing in a **ring light** as a basic light source. They are quite popular and not too expensive; you can get an effective one with a stand for less than $50 online and it will be well worth it even if you only have one virtual meeting a month. A ring light is a circular LED light that is in the shape of a ring (hence ring light). They usually have a few different brightness settings and are quite portable and easy to carry/move around and even pack up with you for travel. They are pretty sufficient on their own, but I suggest using them with natural and overhead lighting to add texture.

If you are participating in virtual meetings more frequently, let's say on a daily basis or even a couple times a week, you may want to think about a more sophisticated set up. A **three-point lighting set up**; this involves 3 lights in a kind of triangle configuration. A **key light**, a **fill light** and a **back light**. The **key light** is the brightest light and just off to one side of the camera, the **fill light** is mirroring the key light on the opposite side to fill in any shadows, the **back light** is shining from behind to give a sense of depth. Below is a diagram explaining the set up:

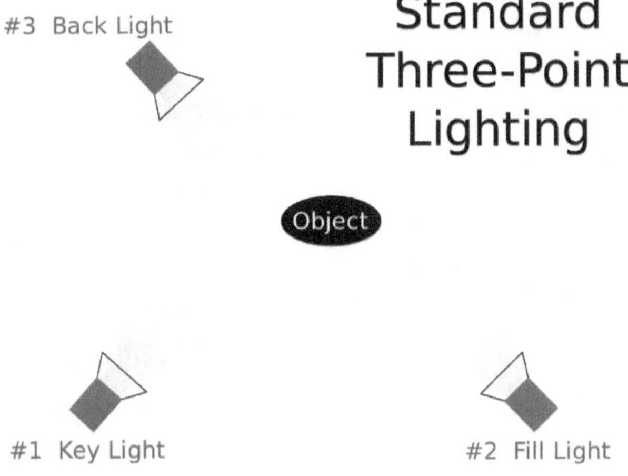

There are several affordable 3-light packages available online that come with stands starting around $100. This may be a worthwhile investment for you if, for example, you will be making multiple virtual sales appointments on a daily basis, if you are a team leader who is interacting multiple times a day, or if you are in senior management and need to maintain your status. In today's world there are plenty of affordable resources available, and this is where the future of business is headed, there is no longer an excuse to avoid stepping up your game.

Once you have decided on what lighting setup best suits your needs, spend some time testing it out. Try your **ring light** or **three-point**

setup with and without overhead light and/or lamps. If you have an amazing natural light source experiment with adding the lights in the room and the ring light to see what is most effective (remember this natural light source is inconsistent and you will need options for cloudy days).

If you have incorporated natural light into your lighting set up make sure you give yourself at least 20 minutes to work on the lighting before your meeting, since natural light is inconsistent and can vary even minute to minute.

When using only controlled light sources, make specific notes about your set up and light settings to cut down the amount of time it takes to recreate the same results each time. If you have the luxury or space and need this equipment daily, maybe you can leave the **setup** to live in the meeting **location**.

Totally not as complicated as you thought it would be; just a little bit of time, a quick ring light purchase and voila! Now, you're ready for your close-up!

Questions to consider:

Does your residence/office have good natural light?

What lighting do you have access to? Will this be enough?

What mood/tone are you trying to set?

Is it time to invest in a *ring light* or *three-point setup*?

STEP # 4

SETUP - FRAME

You are doing great! This is the last step that involves any of the technical aspects of how to set yourself up for mastering your virtual meeting.

The **frame** is what is actually seen through the lens of the camera or on the screen. You may be taking a meeting from your phone or tablet but the people on the other end might be looking at you on a large monitor or even a TV screen. This is definitely something to keep in mind throughout your setup process. You will want to come across as *polished and professional* as possible no matter what size the screen, so always prepare for being seen on the large screen version. Some details that may seem insignificant on a phone or tablet are quite prominent on a larger device.

Once you have a designated **location** and an effective **lighting** setup, you will want to make any necessary adjustments to the picture that appears on your screen - your **frame**.

You don't need to be a professional cinematographer to get this right, all you need is a little guidance and a little patience. In terms of **frame**, I suggest positioning the camera to capture the classic "head and shoulders" shot, which is standard for acting auditions. Basically the top of your head is touching the top of the frame and the bottom of the frame is just below your shoulders, at the top of your armpit crease.

A few common mistakes I see over and over again in meetings and even on TV with virtual guests, is leaving the laptop resting directly on the desk, holding the phone in hand and looking down, or resting the tablet in hand or leaning it on the desk. These practices are fine for casual conversation with friends and family but do not translate in a professional setting. In all of these positions the camera is angled up coming from underneath the face, the individual is looking down at the camera and often the ceiling is visible.

This camera placement is ineffective because 1) the camera is below eye level and 2) the angle can distort depth perception.

No matter what device you use, you will want the camera to be at eye level. So, for example, if you are using a laptop, you can stack a couple of large books, or place a shoe box on your desk and rest the laptop on top, bringing the camera to a higher level in line with your eyes. Like I mentioned in step #3 *eye contact is key to clear communication*. If you are using a phone or a tablet it will be worth your while to invest a few dollars in a stand, the added benefit to that is having your hands free.

If you are using a laptop make sure the camera/screen is at a 90 degree angle with base/keyboard, with a phone or tablet make sure the device is at a 90 degree angle perpendicular to the surface it is resting on. You may adjust the angle a few degrees but this is a neutral starting point, and a less than 90 degree (slightly closed) angle is preferable than a greater angle (slightly open).

Keep the level of your camera in mind when setting up your location, background and your lighting. All the aspects work together to create the desired picture.

Now that you are familiar with the basic setup I'd like to encourage you to take advantage of the opportunity you have to tell a story in your frame.

Questions to consider:

Is your laptop or camera eye level?

Is there anything unwanted, distracting or superfluous in the frame?

Does everything in your frame serve a purpose?

If not, can it be removed or replaced with something more specific?

STEP #5

APPEARANCE

What brand are you (selling)? Do you look the part? In order to master the virtual meeting you will have to pay more attention to specific details that you may not focus on during an "in person" encounter. Close-up and on-camera, a polished (or unpolished appearance) is more noticeable than ever. Just because you and your team, colleagues or clients are at home does not mean that everyday has automatically turned into "casual Friday." As a matter of fact, since you are not in the office or a professional setting your professional appearance becomes that much more important to the success of your interactions. Your work is not casual, your goals are not casual therefore nothing about your interactions should be casual.

Professional actors are aware that actions speak louder than words, and the simple nuances that separate the *working actors* from the *stars* are in their unspoken behavior. According to Dr. Mehrabian's **7-38-55 rule**, the mind determines meaning in three ways: **7 percent** verbal, **38 percent** vocal and **55 percent** visual. That means that **93 percent** of communication is nonverbal. Wow, that's a huge percentage, and this study wasn't even targeted to virtual interactions. Good thing you're taking some time to focus on and refine your nonverbal cues, you are such a pro!

Let's start with **grooming**. No, I don't expect that you will be rolling out of bed in your jammies and signing on to a meeting. But I am assuming that you are probably skipping some steps in your grooming routine since you're not leaving the house. *Don't skip any steps just because you're not leaving the house.* Like the cologne or perfume you like, but don't want to "waste" since no one can smell you. *You can smell you,* and there is a whole sensorial experience you are missing out on when you skip certain parts of your grooming ritual because you aren't interacting in your usual fashion. The steps we take to get ready to go to the office, or for a big meeting or presentation affect our mood and our mindset. You can't afford to skimp on these things if you truly want to master the virtual meeting. Take the shower, do your hair, wear the fragrance, brush and floss, do all the little things just as you would if you were to leave your home. It does make a difference, trust me, maybe not to *them* but it will to *you.* And that translates on camera.

Next, I want to talk about **wardrobe**, as we call it in the performance world. What costume will you be wearing? Yes, costume. We wear different clothing that corresponds to different purposes and activities. We don't wear a cocktail dress to the gym so there is no reason to wear gym shorts or yoga pants to the virtual meeting. *You will know the difference and yes it will affect your performance and presentation.*

One of the most important things I tell my clients is to *wear pants!* Literally. Like real pants that have a button and a zipper and are a little stiffer and less comfortable than sweats, gym clothing or loungewear. You feel differently in pants, you sit differently in pants, and you therefore speak and present differently in pants.

I also insist on wearing shoes, proper shoes not slippers, sandals or sneakers. Once again shoes are a little restrictive, they make you feel differently, sit differently and they bring on a different subconscious awareness.

Prior to meetings going virtual, have you ever gone to a meeting without wearing pants or shoes? Why would you start now? You don't want to appear stiff or uncomfortable but you're also not hanging out with friends chillin' either. There is work to be done, targets to hit, teams to manage and deadlines to make. When you **dress for success** the action is equally about how the costume *makes you feel* than the *impression it gives off*.

Choose to wear colors that are flattering, when testing your setup try on a few different shirts to see what works best. Avoid faded or worn in materials and busy or loud patterns. I would also avoid visible brand labels or logos that are not specific to your company or your goal. You will also want to be aware of how the color looks with your background; if you are presenting in front of a *white* wall, a *white* shirt isn't the best choice.

Have 3-5 solid outfit choices that are your go-to's on hand. When you're prepping for an important presentation the last thing you want to worry about is what to wear.

Now that we've got the outside cover, let's go inside (your head).

Questions to consider:

What brand are you (selling)?

Do you look the part?

What colors look good on you?

What hairstyle frames your face in the most flattering manner ?

How does the lighting (or lack of) affect your appearance?

STEP #6

MENTAL PREP

Alright, you've got your setup and your wardrobe figured out, now it's time to focus on how to mentally prepare for your meeting. As I've mentioned throughout these steps, *mood* and *energy* are crucial components to mastering the virtual meeting. **Grooming** and **wardrobe** have their part to play in getting yourself there, but the outside is just the beginning. Now it's time for the inner work.

Why is **mental preparation** so important? You may be able to hide your mood or true feelings in person but you can't lie or hide on camera. *The camera picks up everything, even your thoughts.* No it can't read minds, but if you're in a negative mood, the camera will see it the camera will see it in your eyes, in they way the muscles in your face tense up, the way you clench your jaw, the insincerity of your smile; that's why mental preparation is so important.

There is something about being in a room with people that gets us going, we are able to feed off of other people's energy and it helps us get excited and inspired. Since this is not possible in the virtual meeting, we have to find different ways to get ourselves pumped before we sign into the meeting.

There are several tricks actors use to get themselves in the mood for a particular scene. Here I will talk about three different techniques you can use to help enhance your mood and increase energy prior to your virtual meeting: **visualization**, **physical activity**, and **solo dance party**.

Visualization: sit quietly for 10 minutes (or more) and visualize the most successful outcome you can imagine for the meeting. Start off with your eyes closed breathing in and out normally through your nose. Imagine the ideal setting for the meeting and who you are meeting with. Think about your talking points in the order you will be discussing them. Slowly go through each talking point or order of business and with each one imagine an overwhelmingly positive response as you go through the list. Let your imagination fuel your excitement and experience the sensation in your body. Please note, this is different from rehearsing your presentation; during a rehearsal you will be focused on *what you do*, in the visualization, your concern is how you desire *others will react*.

Visualization is not effective for everyone, maybe you are more of a **physical activity** person. If you have a chance to workout or hit the gym before the meeting that is ideal. If not, you can still do a few things in your home to get the blood and ideas flowing. Try doing 3 sets of 10 push-ups, 3 sets of twenty jumping jacks, or even jogging on the spot a few minutes prior to the meeting. You don't want to get sweaty and disheveled, you just want to do enough to get the heart pumping to increase your energy level.

The next one is my personal favorite, a **solo dance party**. This should be pretty straight forward; put on a few of your favorite songs that always *put a smile on your face* and *get your energy up* and rock out to them (no depressing, sad or slow music). Celebrate your awesomeness, the success this meeting will bring and the simple fact that you are alive and able to dance. Remind yourself how blessed you are for the opportunity to meet with the wonderful people on the other side of the screen. **Even if you don't necessarily feel this way, dance it out until you do, because the camera is unforgiving and can see all those negative thoughts in your eyes and on your face and there is no room for negativity if you're gonna master this virtual meeting!**

Feel free to try any combination of these techniques that suit you, or if you have other things that work for you, do those (and please share them with me, I'm always happy to learn about new tricks that can help increase energy and positivity).

Now that you're in the groove, time to make your meeting smooth.

Questions to consider:

How do you feel?

Are you excited to interact with the people you're meeting with?

Do you have lots of energy?

Are you pumped up?

STEP #7

PRESENTATION: SMILE, YOU'RE ON CAMERA

You're all set up, looking sharp, and ready to roll. Now it's time to go over some specifics for how to best present in an on-camera close-up.

As I mentioned before, 93% of communication is nonverbal, and 55% of that is attributed to body language. That's why mental prep and getting in the right mindset is crucial, because just like the camera, the body doesn't lie. So here are a few tips that will help ensure your **presentation** is effective and memorable:

First of all you'll want to be aware of your **posture**. Sitting up straight, forward towards the front edge of your chair, with your feet planted on the ground is best; this is an active and activating position that allows you to stay energetic. It's best to avoid leaning against the back of your chair, this can cut off the flow of energy and look lazy. Try not to cross your legs so your feet stay grounded and rooted on the floor. If your feet don't reach the floor completely (like in my case) place a box of a few books on the ground so you can plant your feet.

Work at becoming aware of any fidgeting, shifting in your seat, crossing and uncrossing your legs, looking down at other things on your desk, touching your face, biting or tensing your lip, and any other physical habits you may not be conscious of. You will want to stay alert and engaged for the entire meeting, even when you are not speaking. Since you can't control how other people are viewing the meeting, you never know when someone will click on your image and have your face across their screen.

The second thing to be aware of is your **voice**. You'll want to articulate yourself clearly with enough volume. Remember 38% of communication is *tone of voice*. Speak with energy but be aware that you're not talking too fast even when excited , you don't want anything you're discussing to get missed. Don't be afraid to speak from a place of power and authority, if you didn't have something important to communicate you wouldn't be included in the meeting.

Also, remember to be patient when listening and responding to others, to avoid any overlap or cutting people off before they are finished their thought. Sometimes in a virtual meeting with many people it's hard to pick up on when someone is finished speaking, so better to have a few seconds of thoughtful silence than talking over someone.

If you find you often run out of air when talking, trip over your words when thinking too fast or would like to improve your vocal tone in general, it is a good idea to practice using your breath and your voice. Some simple **breathing exercises** can help you become aware of breathing a little deeper so you don't run out of air when speaking. **Articulation exercises** and **tongue twisters** can help with preventing tripping over words. **Resonance exercises** can help improve vocal tone in general. I have included some exercises on pages .... to help you overcome these issues.

The third thing I want to suggest you bring to your meeting is **emotion**. If you are not emotionally charged when speaking you will not affect the people listening to you no matter how important, accurate or interesting your presentation is. Humans are emotional beings, and emotion is what drives our actions. In order for anyone to take action because of what you're saying they need to have some sort of emotional connection specific to you or your purpose.

One trick that can help you bring emotion to your meeting is by choosing your **intentions** and writing them down. I suggest writing down an intention next to each talking point to keep your presentation dynamic. For example, if you are a team leader trying to drive more sales in your department these could be some effective intentions: Maybe you begin with **praise** (people always respond well to appreciation), next you may want to **inspire** your team with a story or anecdote about someone overcoming the market against all odds, finally you will conclude by **motivating** them with a vision of what the future will look like once the goal is achieved. Of course motivation was the intention from the beginning, but, do you see how each intention builds on the previous one to take the team on an emotional journey? I have included a list of active verbs and intentions on pages 33-35 as a tool to help you choose your intentions and make your meeting effective on an emotional level by emotionally activating those you are meeting with.

The fourth thing I want to mention, is to **smile**, not a huge fake grin, just a subtle one (unless it's completely inappropriate). We always come across better on a close-up with a smile, even if it's just in the eyes.

The last thing I suggest is to **record and watch** a rehearsal of your presentation (or even recite a poem or a few verses of a song in your natural speaking voice). I understand this is difficult for most people, it's hard to watch ourselves on camera. But if you're going to master these skills it's important to be aware of how you look, sound and come across on screen. The virtual meeting is being accepted as the new norm across the globe and mastering your skills will only put you ahead of the game.

If it's possible to record an actual meeting I suggest you do so as well, the more aware you are of your presence, behavior and voice the more command you will have of refining your skills and making deliberate choices. It is also effective to watch others in the meeting and make note of who are strong and weak presenters and why. Oftentimes it's easier to learn from someone else's good and bad habits instead of our own, because we can be too harsh and self-critical with ourselves.

Be easy on yourself and don't get discouraged. Even professional actors mess up a bunch. It's normal even for people who make millions of dollars performing on camera. If you get down on yourself just go to YouTube and watch a blooper reel from one of your favorite shows. You'll see, this stuff is challenging even for the hot shots; they forget their lines, trip over words and make all the same mistakes you might... because at the end of the day they're also human and just trying their best to do a good job.

Remember that you're awesome and determined and you'll get through it cause your work is important.

The last thing I want to mention is to be mindful of **distractions** that can arise. Make sure the people you share space with are aware of the meeting, how long it will run, and that you will need *silence and privacy* for that duration of time. A pet lurking in the background is always adorable and entertaining, but can and will steal focus from you and your presentation, so it's best to have pets in another room if possible.

I know you weren't crazy about venturing into the brave new virtual business world at first, but now that I've broken it down simply, isn't it kind of exciting? Just follow the steps and you're gonna do great. You'll even get better and better each time you work at it! I believe in you.

Questions to consider:

Are you sitting upright in an energetic position?

How do you sound?

Do you have clear intentions to make your meeting effective emotionally?

Did you record and watch yourself rehearse?

Did you notice any physical or vocal habits you were not aware of?

Is there anything specific you know you have trouble with?

What would you like to improve on?

Breathing Exercises: For Running Out Of Air

Breathing Set Up:

The best way to get started is to lie down on the floor if that's accessible to you (if not sitting upright in a chair will also work). Lie on your back with a book (1-2 inches thick) under your head, your knees bent and feet on the floor. The book is to align your neck so your throat isn't strained from over extending. Rest one hand on your chest and the other on your belly. Imagine the breath filling your belly as well as your chest. We have a much greater breath capacity than we use in everyday life.

Breathing Exercise:

Start off breathing normally for several breaths. Inhale for the count of three, and then exhale for the count of three. Continue this for several breaths.

Next, inhale for the count of five, and then exhale for the count of five. Continue for several breaths.

Repeat this exercise building to 10, 12, 15 and even 20 if you can (of course not all on the same day). Spend about five minutes focusing on your breath.

Resonance Exercises: For Vocal Tone & Quality

Lying Down:

While on your back, in the position explained in "breathing setup", begin vocalizing. Focus on holding the sound as long as you have breath. Don't push and don't strain.

Mmmmmmmmm - Repeat 5-10 times.
Haaaaaaaaaaaa - Repeat 5-10 times.
Maaaaaaaaaaaa - Repeat 5-10 times

Now alternate between Ha and Ma a few times on the same breath.

On a whisper count by thousands from 1000, 2000, 3000 all the way to 10,000. Try building your way up to 15,000.

Standing Up

1) Resonance:

For these exercises you will focus on resonating into different locations in your mouth, chest and head. Hold each sound until you are out of breath, stop when you run out, don't push.
Repeat each sound below three times:

Mmm – feel the vibrations on the lips
Nnn – place tongue behind the teeth

Nng (as in 'sing') – tongue at the roof of your mouth to the back

Haw – feel the resonance in you chest

Ha – feel the vibrations in the back of your head just above your neck

Ngeeeeeng – vibrate in the nasal cavity

Hold the following sounds for 5 seconds, work your way to 10, then 15 seconds:

Zzzzzzzzzz

Sssssssssss

Vvvvvvvvv

2) Lip Trills:

Push air out of the lips like a motorboat sound and hum the count of five. Start with singles then work your way up to doubles (hum 1-5 x 2) and triples (hum 1-5 x 3) all on the same breath. This is a great warm up and for when your voice is tired.

Annunciation & Articulation Exercises

For these exercises, exaggerate the movements of your lips and tongue:

B-B-B-B
BB-BB-BB-BB
BB**B**-BB**B**-BB**B**-BB**B**
BBB**B**-BBB**B**-BBB**B**-BBB**B**

D-D-D-D
DD-DD-DD-DD
DDD-DDD-DDD-DDD
DDDD-DDDD-DDDD-DDDD

G-G-G-G
G**G**-G**G**-G**G**-G**G**
GG**G**-GG**G**-GG**G**-GG**G**
GGG**G**-GGG**G**-GGG**G**-GGG**G**

B D B D B D - D B D B D B (repeat 3 times)
B G B G B G - G B G B G B (repeat 3 times)
D G D G D G - G D G D G D (repeat 3 times)
B D G D B - B D G D B - B D G D B - B D B G D B (repeat 3 times)

V - TH - V - TH - V - TH, TH - V - TH - V - TH V (repeat 3 times)
V - TH - Z, V - TH - Z, V - TH - Z, O V - TH - Z (repeat 3 times)
V - TH - Z - ZH, V - TH - Z - ZH, V - TH - Z -ZH (repeat 3 times)
M – N – NG, M – N – NG, M – N – NG (repeat 3 times)

Bah dah gah pah dah gah
Boh doh goh poh doh goh
Boo doo goo poo doo goo
Bee dee gee pee dee gee
Bay day gay pay day gay

Mah nah lah thah vah zah
Moh noh loh thoh voh zoh
Moo noo loo thoo voo zoo
Mee nee lee thee vee zee
May nay lay thay vay zay

Sah Kah She Fah Rah
Pah Kah She Fah Rah
Wah Kah She Fah Rah
Bah Kah She Fah Rah
Dah Kah She Fah Rah

Muh mah
Muh may
Muh mee
Muh may
Muh mah
Muh MAW
Muh moo
Muh Moh
Muh mah (Repeat replacing M with N, Z, L, T, G, K, P)

Tongue Twisters

Work on repeating these three times fast, three times in a row:

1. Copper Coffee Pot, Copper Coffee Pot, Copper Coffee Pot
2. Choose Orange Shoes, Choose Orange Shoes, Choose Orange Shoes
3. Eleven Benevolent Elephants, Eleven Benevolent Elephants, Eleven Benevolent Elephants
4. Girl Gargoyle, Guy Gargoyle; Girl Gargoyle, Guy Gargoyle; Girl Gargoyle, Guy Gargoyle
5. Lili, Loli, Looli, Lawl; Lili, Loli, Looli, Lawli; Lili, Loli, Looli, Lawli,
6. Literally Literary, Literally Literary, Literally Literary,
7. Many Many Moaning Men, Many Many Moaning Men, Many Many Moaning Men
8. Sushi Chef, Sushi Chef, Sushi Chef
9. Toy Boat, Toy Boat, Toy Boa,
10. Unique New York, Unique New York, Unique New York
11. Red Lemon, Yellow Lemon, Red Lemon, Yellow Lemon
12. Around the rocks the ragged rascal ran
13. Wandering and wondering they wend their way around the river bend
14. She sells seashells by the sea shore
15. The big black bug bit the itty bitty baby
16. My cutlery cuts keenly and clean

INTENTIONS

URGE

INCITE

PUSH

INDUCE

NULLIFY

GUIDE

STUN

RESIST

PUT ON ICE

CATCH THE EYE

SOLVE PROBLEM

KEEP GOING

REALIZE DREAM

PROBE

DERAIL

SWIM AGAINST

FIND
PROTECTION

MAINTAIN MY
DIGNITY

AVOID THE
TRUTH

CHANGE THE
MOOD

KEEP THINGS MY
WAY

FIGURE OUT

PICK UP THE
PIECES

GET
COMPASSION

AWAKEN

STIR

ROUSE

EMBOLDEN

OBLIGE

PRY

SHAPE

FOLLOW

REBEL AGAINST

FIGHT FOR

SUSTAIN

HAVE FUN

INGRATIATE

REPROVE

DEFLATE

DELIGHT

CRITICIZE

CHARM

ALARM

PROVOKE

CONQUER

DELAY

COMPROMISE

PLACATE

LURE

SCOLD

RELAX

ADMONISH

DAZZLE

HUMOR

REFLECT

HURT

CONFRONT

DEMAND

PLEAD

IMPLORE

PROTEST

COMMAND

DOMINATE

IMPRESS

MYSTIFY

BEWITCH

INTRIGUE

PLEASE

ACTIVE VERBS

ACKNOWLEDGE	CONFRONT	ENGULF
ACTIVATE	CONJURE	ENLIST
AGREE WITH	CONQUER	ENLIVEN
ALARM	CONSOLE	ENTERTAIN
ALLEVIATE	CONTEST	ENTHRALL
ALLURE	CONTRADICT	ENTHUSE
ALLY	CONVERT	ENTICE
ALTER	CORRECT	ENTREAT
ANIMATE	COUNTER	EXALT
APOLOGIZE	COVER	EXCITE
APPEAL	CRITICIZE	EXCLUDE
APPRAISE	DAZZLE	EXPLOIT
AWAKEN	DEFEND	FACE UP
BEDAZZLE	DEFLATE	FASCINATE
BEFRIEND	DEFLECT	FEED
BRIGHTEN	DEFY	FIGHT
BUTTER UP	DELAY	FIND
CAJOLE	DELIGHT	PROTECTION
CALM	DEMAND	FLATTER
CAPTIVATE	DISARM	FLAUNT
CAPTURE	DOMINATE	FOLLOW
CAUTION	EASE	FOOL
CHALLENGE	EDUCATE	FORCE
CIRCUMVENT	ELEVATE	FOSTER
CLAIM	EMBRACE	FREE
COAX	EMPLOY	HYPNOTIZE
COERCE	EMPOWER	IGNITE
COMFORT	ENCHANT	IMMERSE
COMMAND	ENCOURAGE	IMPASSION
CONFOUND	ENERGIZE	IMPLORE
	ENGAGE	IMPRESS

IMPROVE
INCITE
INFUSE
INGRATIATE
INSPIRE
INSTILL
INTRIGUE
INVIGORATE
INVOLVE
LEAD
LIBERATE
LOOSEN-UP
MANEUVER
MENTOR
MOTIVATE
NURTURE
OBJECT
OBLIGE
OBLITERATE
ORDER
OVERWHELM
PACIFY
PERK UP
PERSUADE
PLACATE
PLAY
PLEAD
PLEASE
PRAISE
PRESS
PRESSURE
PREVAIL
PRIME

PROBE
PROD
PROTECT
PROVOKE
PRY
PSYCHE UP
PULL TOGETHER
PUMP UP
PURSUE
PUSH
PUT AT EASE
QUESTION
QUIET
REASON WITH
REASSURE
REBEL
REFLECT
RELAX
RELEASE
RELIEVE
RISE ABOVE
REPAIR
REPROVE
RESPOND
RETALIATE
REVEAL
ROUSE
SAVE
SELL
SERVE
SET STRAIGHT
SHAKE
SHAPE

SHINE
SHOCK
SMOOTH
SOFTEN
SOOTHE
STAND UP TO
STIMULATE
STIR
STRENGTHEN
STUN
SUBDUE
SUPPORT
SURMOUNT
SUSTAIN
SWIM AGAINST
TURN THE
TABLES
UNMASK
URGE
WAKE THEM UP
WARN
WIN OVER
TAKE IN HAND
TEACH

About The Author

Jennifer Lieberman is an award-winning writer/performer and producer from Maple, Ontario, Canada. After years of pounding the pavement and knocking on doors with no success of breaking into the entertainment industry, she decided to take matters into her own hands and created the solo-show "Year of the Slut". This show proved to be her break and the play "Year of the Slut" is now the novel "Year of the What?"

Since deciding to "make her own break" Lieberman has appeared in over 30 international stage productions and has produced over 40 independent film and theatre productions. She has penned a number of stage and screen plays and her short films have screened at the Festival de Cannes among other international festivals. She is currently gearing up to direct her first feature film.

Jennifer founded Make Your Own Break to help others take control of their creative careers by providing the tools to learn how to produce independent productions with little to no resources. For more information about her workshops and one-on-one consulting opportunities please visit www.MakeYourOwnBreak.com.